Where Indians Live:
American Indian Houses

by Nashone

Illustrations by Louise Smith

Sierra Oaks Publishing Company
1989

Other Children's Books By Sierra Oaks Publishing Company:

Grandmother's Christmas Story: A True Quechan Indian Story
A Trip to a Pow Wow
Grandmother Stories of the Northwest
Grandfather's Origin Story: The Navajo Indian Beginning
Grandfather's Story of Navajo Monsters
A, B, C's The American Indian Way
Creation of a California Tribe: Grandfather's Maidu Indian Tales

Copyright © 1989

Sierra Oaks Publishing Company
P.O. Box 255354
Sacramento, California   95865-5354

ISBN: 0-940113-16-3

To my husband and daughters, with love

2

Indians built the first houses in America. They built their houses in mountains and caves. These houses are called cliff dwellings. It was not easy to reach these houses. The Indians who lived in the cliff houses used ladders to climb into their houses. They had to step carefully so they wouldn't fall off the mountain.

Some Indians lived where it was very cold. Their homes
were built to keep the cold outside. An igloo is made out of blocks of
ice, but it is warm inside. Eskimos make igloos today.

These Inuit or Eskimo girls lived in an Igloo. The girl on the left is wearing her hair in a special way. Her mother wrapped her hair around sticks and tied it with strips of caribou skin.

    Other Indians lived where it was very hot. This is a drawing
of a Tohono O'Odham or Papago house, which was made out of
both plants and earth. These Indians lived in the desert. They used
wood from cactus plants to make the ceiling. Then they put mud
on the outside. This kept the house very cool.

Matthew Ignacio, Joshua Stern, and Jazzmine Stern are
Tohono O'Odham. Their people, known to others as Papagos, live
in southern Arizona. The children enjoy learning about the
culture and traditions of their elders.

7

Some Indians lived where it rained a lot. They needed a house that stayed dry inside. The Miwok Indians used plants to weave thick mats. These mats made the walls of some houses.

Miwok children grew up in well-made houses. These Miwoks are members of Bill Franklin's Miwok dance group. The picture was taken in front of the California State Indian Museum in Sacramento, California.

Other Indians lived on flat land. The Navajo Indians were sheep ranchers. Many Navajos still raise sheep. A hogan is a Navajo house. It usually has eight sides. The door entering the hogan must always face east.

Navajo people lived in hogans. These children look on as
their mothers spin and weave wool. The women make beautiful
rugs.

Houses built by Indians were sometimes small. The Apache
wickiup is one of the smallest houses built by Indians. These
houses were used mostly for sleeping.

Apache boys and girls grew up in wickiups. Chief Geronimo
lived in such a home when he was young. Geronimo was a famous
war leader from Arizona and New Mexico.

Other Indian houses were big. These houses were used for many things. The Indians would sleep, cook, and tell stories in these big houses. This is a Sac-Fox bark house.

Keokuk was a Sac chief from Illinois. He fought against the British during the War of 1812. He was a friend of the Americans. President James Monroe awarded him the Peace Medal seen around his neck.

Many Indian houses were round in shape. This picture shows a wigwam. The Indians who built wigwams lived where it was cold and windy. They built fires to keep the wigwams warm inside.

This family called themselves Anishinaabeg. Other people named them Chippewa or Ojibway Indians. Around 1925, Tom and Mary Wind and their baby posed for this picture in front of a store at Wigwam Bay.

But other Indian houses were not round. The Iroquois people lived in longhouses. Two or three families lived in each house. Each family had an area inside the longhouse that was their own place to live.

18

Cornplanter was a Seneca Indian chief. The Senecas were one of the six Iroquois tribes. Cornplanter and other Indians from the Eastern woodlands lived in longhouses. Iroquois people still use the longhouse.

Some Indians moved around from place to place. They needed houses that could move with them. The tipi was made out of wooden poles and buffalo skins. Women took down the tipis when the Indians had to leave their camp. Women also put up the tipis at the new camp.

Anna Puzz is an Assiniboin woman whose people lived on the Northern Plains. Like many Indians on the Great Plains, Anna's people lived in tipis that were often painted with pictures of people, animals, and designs.

Not all Indians moved around. Some Indians stayed in the same place all year long. They built houses that could not be moved. Hopi Indians lived in small villages. Their houses were built close to each other. They were made out of mud, rocks, and wood. Many Hopis live in these houses today.

Paul and Paulette Coochyamptewa live in Flagstaff, Arizona, near the Hopi Reservation. Many Hopi, Tewa, and other Pueblo Indians live in homes made of stones, adobe, and timbers. Others return to their villages to visit relatives and to attend ceremonies.

Indians used different kinds of things to build their houses. The Mandan Indians lived in large houses made of mud from the earth. When the mud was dry, it made the walls hard. The Mandan houses were huge inside. More than one family could live in each house.

Shakoka was a Mandan woman who had beautiful flowing grey hair. George Catlin sketched Shakoka at her village on the upper Missouri River in North Dakota. Her home was so large that horses could live in her home with the people.

Other Indians used plants to make their houses. Palouse Indian women wove thick mats from long, thin plants. The mats were placed against the long poles to form the walls. Other poles leaned against the mats on the outside to make the walls strong. The poles kept the wind from blowing the mats away.

Boys and girls among many tribes on the Northwest Plateau lived in mat lodges. This Yakima girl is wearing a buckskin dress, beaded cape, and white necklace. She grew up in a mat lodge. Plateau Indians held ceremonies in some mat lodges.

Sometimes Indians built houses that nobody lived in. This is a Maidu Indian ceremonial building. It was used for special events. Indians danced, drummed, and sang in this kind of house. The Maidu Indians live in northern California. The ceremonial house is important to them today.

Johnny Bob was born and raised in a traditional home of the Maidu Indians. Dancing, singing, and ceremonies were held in the Ceremonial House within his community. Johnny attended the Maidu Bear Dance each year.

Today Indians live in many different kinds of houses. Some Indians live in modern houses. They live in homes that are big and some homes that are small. Just like you and me, Indians live in many kinds of houses!

Indian children live in many kinds of houses today. Skye Williams is an Assiniboin Indian who lives in a modern-day home in Santee, California. He likes old Indian stories about monsters.

GLOSSARY

Apache Indians live primarily in the deserts and mountains of Arizona and New Mexico, although some Apache bands inhabited regions of Mexico.

Cliff Dwellings are homes built in cave-like overhangings in the sides of mountains. These homes were built over two thousand years ago by ancient Pueblo Indians in the American Southwest.

Hogans are Navajo houses. There are two types of hogans. The "female" hogan is usually designed with eight sides, whereas the "male" hogan is conical in shape. The doorways of both types of hogans face the east in accordance with Navajo tradition. Before a hogan is lived in, it is blessed by a medicine man.

Igloo is an ice house made by the Inuit people, commonly known as Eskimos. The Inuits once lived from the east coast of Canada to the west coast of Alaska. Igloos are still built today, especially when the people are hunting and fishing for long periods of time.

Iroquois originally consisted of five great nations. They formed the Iroquois Confederacy or League in upstate New York and Pennsylvania, as well as in Canada. The tribes included the Seneca, Onondaga, Oneida, Cayuga, and Mohawk. Later, a sixth tribe was added, the Tuscarora.

Maidu is a tribal name meaning "person." The Maidu Indians lived along the Feather and American Rivers in northern California. They still live in the foothills of the Sierra Nevada Mountains.

Mandans are Great Plains Indians who lived in North Dakota along the Missouri River. In the winter of 1804, Meriwether Lewis and William Clark lived with the Mandans and met Sacajewea.

Miwok Indians lived in three distinct areas of California. The major group lived on the western slopes of the Sierra Nevada Mountains in north-central California and along the deltas of the Sacramento and San Joaquin Rivers. Some Miwoks lived near Clear Lake, and others between the Golden Gate and Sonoma Creek, California.

Navajos are the largest Indian tribe in North America, numbering approximately 175,000 people. They also retain the largest land mass, located primarily in northeastern Arizona and northwestern New Mexico.

Palouses once lived along the Snake River in eastern Washington. These people are now located on the Yakima, Nez Perce, Umatilla, and Colville Reservations.

Pueblo means "town" or "village" in Spanish. It is a general name for those Indians in the Southwest who live in villages comprised of stone houses built on mesa tops. One of the Pueblo tribes includes the Hopis. The Hopis have the oldest continuously inhabited village in North America.

Sac-Fox Indians once lived in large homes in Illinois. They farmed the rich soil and hunted game in the woods of the Midwest. Today most of the Sac-Fox people live in Oklahoma.

Tipis are a house built by Great Plains tribes. Tipis were originally made out of buffalo hide and wooden poles. Today canvas is used to make tipis.

Tohono O'Odham, also known as Papago Indians, live in southern Arizona, especially near Tucson, Arizona. Today the Tohono O'Odham are noted for their beautiful and artistic basketry.

Wickiups were temporary homes built by the Apaches out of sticks, brush, and hides. A number of wickiups could be found in established camps or *rancherias*.

Wigwams are round houses built by Indians living near the Great Lakes. The Ojibway or Chippewas made wigwams out of bark, and they were very well-insulated to keep out the cold wind of that region. Some Indians in Canada build wigwams today.

PHOTO CREDITS

Page 5: From Knud Rasmussen, *Intellectual Culture of the Hudson Bay Eskimos*, 1930.

Page 7: Photos by Carmella Ignacio.

Page 9: Courtesy of Ralph and Lisa Shanks, *American Indian Travel Guide*, 1986.

Page 11: Courtesy Navajo Community College.

Page 13: Courtesy Bureau of American Ethnology, Smithsonian Institution.

Page 15: Courtesy Bureau of American Ethnology, Smithsonian Institution.

Page 17: Courtesy Minnesota Historical Society.

Page 19: From Thomas L. McKenney and James Hall, *The Indian Tribes of North America*, 1933.

Page 21: Photo by David Curle.

Page 23: Photo by the author.

Page 25: From George Catlin, *Letters and Notes on the Manners, Customs, and Condition of the North American Indians*, 1841.

Page 27: Courtesy of the Yakima Valley Regional Library.

Page 29: Courtesy of the American Museum of Natural History.

Page 31: Photo by David Curle.